Cloud of Ink

Cloud of Ink

L. S. Klatt

University of Iowa Press | Iowa City

University of Iowa Press, Iowa City 52242
Copyright © 2011 by L. S. Klatt
www.uiowapress.org
Printed in the United States of America

Text design by April Leidig-Higgins

The University of Iowa Press is a member of Green
Press Initiative and is committed to preserving
natural resources.

Printed on acid-free paper

ISBN-13: 978-1-58729-971-1
ISBN-10: 1-58729-971-2
LCCN: 2010936669

For Kent, Imogene, Kevin, Brian, & all the first teachers

Acknowledgments

"Transit of the Beautiful" and "Liquefaction" first appeared in *Boston Review*; "Cortona," "Husbandry," and "Crete" in *Verse*; "Ovation" in *Drunken Boat*; "A Better Mousetrap" and "King Salmon" in the *Cincinnati Review*; "Semiconductors in the Breadbasket" and "A Sudden Unspeakable Indignation" in *Eleven Eleven*; "Mercy Planet" and "She Makes Me Lie Down" in *Slope*; "Shakedown in the Sugar Shine" in *Parthenon West Review*; "Audubon" in *Sycamore Review*; "Andrew Wyeth, Painter, Dies at 91" in the *Believer*; "George Keats" and "Where My Sunflower Wishes to Go" in *JERRY*; and "The Pear as a Wild Boar" as a broadside by the Kalamazoo Book Arts Center.

Contents

In my room, the world is beyond my understanding;

But when I walk I see that it consists of three or four hills and a cloud.

— Wallace Stevens

Cloud of Ink

Aeronautics

Whereupon you are alone
in a cockpit, a multitude behind you sealed tight,

& it occurs to you that you are in an updraft
of ampersands & colophons. Very well,

you have trimmed lassitude into a jet
that bears you & others into a stratosphere yet to be

graphed; the date of your death you do not know
nor do you assume it is ascertainable forthwith

but skyward the flyer, folded in half, of blue wove
paper. The plane fights, aligns itself in nebula.

MORE SPLENDID

Picasso has never seen the earth
from an airplane. If
from below, Lorca
can imagine the elderly
Picasso as a wing-walker
that would be faith. That
would be a tabula rasa
on which to describe a bowl
of lemons. The whole world waits
for Picasso to cube a guitar
or pink it with shears until watermelon.
Carrying the coffin, Picasso wishes
that Lorca was made
of balsa wood.

LIQUEFACTION

I found an octopus in the snow.

And not knowing what it was or why it was there, I gutted it
as if a hunter.

To me, up to my elbows in bladder, the ink was a surprise.

I wore it like opera gloves in the moonlight.

So many mistook my passion for gangrene.

One followed me into an orchestra pit. If I could only say now
what my arms said.

I took up a bassoon & aimed it at a chandelier.

As the house lights came down, the audience lost their places.

They were swimming in a maelstrom of inklings.

Transit of the Beautiful

Cockroach on the lip
of a teacup

while the woman upstairs

puts a bag over her head
& gasses the house.

In conclusion, the lights go out; the soul is denuded.

The insect makes no attempt to be heard
no scream

but, antennae waving like palm fronds before the Prince
of Peace, crawls into the cup.

To be destroyed, to be indestructible,
this is always the question.

INSULT IS NECESSARY FOR THE PERFECTION OF BEAUTY

Heads of lavender spit at damselflies.

This is not hate but a byword.
As it is written . . .

The winged shall be perfumed in gardens.

Here on the page, a bluebottle swivels,
the fly

a cursor that eschews lines

& quiet feet leave sticky notes
for a sonata.

Emerson revised:

wise moments are fire-
flies that scar the countenance ever.

MOMENTUM

With this thread I tie myself to the fly
for let us share chromosomes. I also drag
behind me an iceberg on leash & our fondness
for consuming. When

I leave the horizon, a pyramid is buried
upside down between dunes. Big lake, it tastes
like a fried egg, a blue one. One

by one, the glaciers are grazed upon. But of
my own effacement, I pause for a moment
of clarity.

ANDREW WYETH, PAINTER, DIES AT 91

A weathered barn on a hilltop; a nude woman
sprawled on the slope
below.

A giant squid rises out of a hayfield, & the barn
is compassed in tentacles
then a cloud of ink.

A man with a fountain pen in his hand
& a pitchfork
in his back

walks the cow-path around the barn
& tells the beauty
on the hill

to step to it. It's as if her freckled skin
is newly charcoaled
& the hayloft

a smokescreen. The cows can't be heard for certain
within the inkblot
but deer

creep to the edge of the field on
delicate feet.

The Pear as a Wild Boar

The hunter, who spent the better part of an afternoon
tracking spoor, now comes upon the wounded pear
& puts fingers to neck

&, feeling
the pace of its breath, slits its throat.

He dresses the slain in a field
where the skins of others are strung from a tree
& looks up at the tusk of a crescent moon.

It has been a day of horrific slaughter,
every sense sated, & what if

to consider the roseate fruit
he lies down with it
as last light caresses hips & rib cage?

The shapeliness of this final punctuation is not meant to pose
a question, merely a respite until the hunter is overtaken
by sleep

& dreams again of game,
the postulate sought, infinity.

HUSBANDRY

At the University Swine Center
the razorbacks present pristine rumps
— they fight to be hosed.

The horseflies too are clean
& green glorious,
as if the shit here
is full of fruit & fiber.

Thus I will have to steal it,
secrete it,
tell it my sad, unctuous story.

Ohio

I worry about your fences

wherein thousands of propane tanks
stand breast to breast
like white chickens.

Chickens
depend on wishbones

& their smelly parts set off alarms
near Dayton.

Those that range
cross I-75 where they are struck
now & then by Airstreams.

So much attention here given to the tornado.

I would like to add that when threatened
chickens retreat into silos.

It makes sense, if it's true, that Ohio
is the birthplace of flight.

BERRYMAN IN CINCINNATI

A very pleasant city except for the cicadas
which crash-landed. After seventeen years
underground, a horde was born
outnumbering its predation. So, as I
was saying, a very pleasant city in spite
of the acoustics. Those were days
when in all my dreaminess
I could play no nocturne & I amplified
underground. For I was a dead
Berryman, & I ferried the souls
of the dispossessed across the Ohio.
There I met the ibis, its plumage a white
paintbrush. And with it I erased what I
knew was melody without hope
of noisemaking. That was a sign,
was it the last, that the lyre would be
heavy metal.

Darwin's Mouth

And out of the mouth
the beetle rides an acrid river
of spittle.

Having
embittered the palate, it returns
to the rainforest, a rare

specimen with three sets of wings:
one covers the face,
one the feet, & with the last

it flies. The scarab hides a lantern
in the banana
leaf

where it waits considering
suitors for its
jade light. No matter the jaguar

or the sloth
the beetle recesses into sanctum
&, all but forgotten, finds

itself next to impossible.

The Zoo of Reason

Under an artificial mist
the platypus
exposes its private parts
to the doubtful. Its snout
is a sensory organ
that wags

&, near the ankle, a spur
is so ready with venom
that merely by
watching
I become a frogman,
an egg-layer.

The plasma
of the fluorescent
light hereafter
floods the habitat
where my mind's been
known

to black out. In
my job as a zookeeper
there are many eyes.
If it were not so
I would say
yes to so
few.

OVATION

The Oval occupies the mind; it does whatever it pleases.

Wherefore, the Hindenburg docks with the Goodyear

& killer whales bump like a bathtub
full of watermelons

& the bathyscaph nurses at the mother ship as a beehive
at the pear tree

& the hedgehog kisses a quail egg. Selah.

.   .   .   .   .

Alleluia. The eyes of the Oval roam to & fro across the face
of the earth

& rest in the feathers of the peacock

& lie on every spreadsheet.

Come & see the acacia leaves that applaud the great neck
of the giraffe.

These are what grew out of the mouth of the Oval.

SHAKEDOWN IN THE SUGAR SHINE

𝄢 & 𝄞
pasted on fenders.
Wings in the blades of windshield wipers.

The Suburban, so adorned, sweats
as a carriage
of kings.

Bees swarm the staves

itching to eat off chrome, itching
to glean the hood.

Dust off the pollen, the infinitesimals,
trick out the rig in woofers
boom boom

— that's enough, that's enough.

Ditch the honey truck; wipe down
the music.

RECREATION

Cloud, you drift above Minnesota,

a thunderhead in the sky unmapped
by meteorologists.

You who watch below

the liquid Minnesotans
& send your glass assassins

to the rusty

have also opened a Rest Area
for Winnebagos

which caravan into heaven.

Cloud of our ancestors
welcome now the Suburbans

for they consume the golden prairie

& they wash in the Mississippi
as if the River of Life.

WHIPPOORWILL

The Blue Ridge in West
Virginia. Mist

covers the whole sleepy thought of it,
including the deer, its black lips

sewn shut with piano wire. Now
we have the beginning
of a hollow

in which a piano tuner searched
for, but failed to find,

the holy ghost.

The longer mystified
the more he was inclined

to silence. There is a thought that one
can hear the whippoorwill
in the muzzle
of a gun.

I never believed that.

The Calm of a Thoughtful Sentence

When you sense a misfire in the brain
it's wistful to seize upon a yak, neck-deep
in the Yangtze, its oblong head serene
as the Himalayas

or to commandeer a kayak in the River
that runs amber, a golden
ox tail that switches
only occasionally

or, lightning bolts notwithstanding, to lasso
the scud that blows West
to East & East
to West

until settled upon the Matterhorn
you feign an alpine meadow
where the how now brown cow
relaxes its insubordinate
hindquarters.

THE GOOD FIGHT

All the fathers gather in the back
of the B-17 bomber. They have volunteered
for death, but now that it's time

to jump, they are unwilling. Thus they huddle
in congregation, training themselves
to cry out, which is a way to navigate when

marooned. And that must be hell, the oblivion
to which nothing aspires, not the Hollywood
jumpers, not the desperate that jerk upward.

And so maybe they fall into deep sleep, neither up
nor down, keeping their half-lives in limbo,
no strings attached. I am talking

about my father who lingered seven years ago
in hospice, a cancer patient. I wasn't there; I was
helpless in another plane, perhaps a cross.

AFFLICTION

I am painting this house with water,
dipping my brush

in clarity, & if I told you the house
is an aquarium

& if I told you the house

is buoyant, would you see
through it?

.　　　.　　　.　　　.　　　.

My house underwater seems misshapen

&, given its tonnage, grotesquely
immersed.

Come to the window, moon
jellyfish. Parachute

of tentacles to outer space.

February

A little girl died
& they laid her in an ambulance
without lights or sirens
because she was already cold.

Some coroner, I suppose, will examine her
& run his thumbs over shinbones.

When I look at the moon, I see the forehead
of a steelworker
creased.

It's a gibbous moon.

In the sink, I wash a bunch of carrots
that have iced
in the crisper. So bright

they look like they should never die.

This neck of the woods, at this time
of year, is as red as ketchup. The light
grows longer; there are
57 varieties.

A Vague Field for Priestcraft

The smudge on your forehead, I consider it a cloud over a skater
on a frozen pond.

In the cloud, a goose is sucked into a jet engine.

But first the nose of the jet entered as a missile.

And that is why, with exit wound, you speak to me of marksmen
as if a tracer got in your head.

I admit that I am searching for a blade
that figures the ice. A scar
seems a necessary evil, while the compulsory, an irritant,
pushes the skater
to the margins.

So that the blade runs out of surface. Near scattershot to find
here a boat made of cinders.

MERCY PLANET

It snowed on Palm Sunday,
olive branches collapsed,
& a stink bug squared himself
inside the windowpane
stuck in condensation.

Feelers looked to the corner
where a recluse deleted an Umbrian
rhyme;
underside faced outward
& became glass-
bottomed
if only to be looked through
to violet.

Hoods of the *misericordia*
laid in a pile
waiting to be used.

Oxidized, the rood
pierced my skull
like a thermometer in roast beef.

CORTONA

My halo attracts lightning
& so I am dead

or possibly there's a dead man
in my mouth

though I'm blowing, blowing
a pigeon to life,

& if not a pigeon
an Etruscan named Dardano.

My city is lit with the snow
of his groin.

Body Part in a Tuscan Garden

We stumble upon a foot,
the pedestal abandoned.

The torso is missing
as is the pelvis; so also the shin.

A foot wrapped in ivy withstands,
has been known to predict a tyrant.

Is it happy? Does it resent?

If a Magdalene waters the toes
what can we surmise from stone?

If a Bernini chisels the heel
is there harm?

Sunlight on footfall presumes so much.

It says to the footloose: remember
the lemon tree.

Canticle : Calculus

Sine & cosine are often invoked.

As when a seeker, I felt for trilobites
in a swift, dark stream.

Anchorites that held — hold me acutely.

Lilies buried by the bulldozer
also fall back on their radicals.

And Pascal, what might you say
to mitochondria that once slept —

you who pose in the scallop
of the baptismal

& still you are impressed
by x?

Extrapolate to the crows, the cows
on their knees

& you get the sense of a greater than
less than.

This wish for triangle.

And there are yet more sides.

ANTEDILUVIAN

The sun spins over the West

a knuckleball. It will never rest,
not in the leaves of the copper beech,

not on the trunk which could be
a brontosaurus leg. Wary

is the H-Bomb; its light
wobbles, feeling ancient. Here come

the Giants. They are not crestfallen;
they pitch their yawps because

the world is swale, the wind blows, the once was
now is, now is not. Was

there ever a reason to think otherwise?

Acqua Alta

A sad iceberg & swamped Venice: a plate
of squid ink, a granule of sugar on the lip.

The Adriatic scribbles in the polygons.
We tourists, too, are signatures. How

many lions stuck on sticks & stones
before espresso cups turn

in their saucers at St. Mark's?

Masons who levitate
square, rhombus, & trapezoid: sink

your hands into the mortar, the smalls
of your backs.

BURANO

Island, whose houses are chromatic, floats
in the Adriatic, an islet

so small it forgot how to swim.
Imagine

this city absorbed in lapis
an inkblot. Say

to the mapmakers: the polis

justifies itself.
Its campanile reaches for a savior, leans.

Reading

In the stern of the sailboat
a god

neither invited nor expected
pilots

a rudder through space.

The sun is not an offense
against majesty

but when it scorches white sails
the hull tips

as if bearing a gold testicle.

That is to say, the universe
is imbalanced

& the moon, in traffic, a whiteness.

For day strip-searches night.

And the orb weighted with itself
wets itself.

WHERE MY SUNFLOWER WISHES TO GO

A goldsmith hammered a sunflower
out of recycled trinkets. It howled

because it was tasteless, because it was
brassy. It could not turn to the sun

like other heliotropes. So the sun

had pity on the yard ornament
& melted it down with ardor.

And the goldsmith soaked his hands
in the liquefaction, & they hardened.

In this condition, he discovered

a finch laying an egg in a trash can.
He could handle neither the bird

nor the egg with his welded fingers.
But the yolk beneath the blue enamel

of the sky made him happy. It cast
his silhouette on the sidewalk while bees

trampled it with mellifluous feet.

OLD WORLD BIRDS

When you talk to the bee-eaters they pretend
you are not there. You can follow them
into Madagascar & across the Mozambique
Channel & still not register
an acknowledgment. This is sad because you
mean no harm & you have taken
great pains to mimic their trills, chuckles,
& whistles. Just to hear Darwin
speak of them, you know that the scythe
of their bills is made for the erratic
snatch of wings midflight, &, as the wings
are indigestible, they eject them. This is
not to say that bee-eaters sugar their songs
with upbeats before disgorging — far
from it. Sometimes they beat the bee
against a branch, then croak. You are
surprised that a diet of stingers yields a rain-
bow plumage, but, given one more reason
to quail, you hardly blush. The mistake
is to imagine on moonlit nights
you are one of them.

White Elephant

Why is it so quiet
in the chamber where I
dress the blind man?
I cloak him in white silk
like snowfall.

An elephant is also
in the room, but, between
the elephant & the blind
man,
I tailor a question.

I think to myself that, even
if the answer is as obvious
as the hand in front
of my face, an imbroglio
is likely to ensue.

As the question
is embroidered, a royal
thread repeats itself,
whereas the truth appears
untouched.

Should the elephant follow
me out of the chamber
& into the rimed
forest, I daresay
this blind man will drift.

ARROW

The Ohio River is in my garage
& a wooly mammoth
distressed by the Stone Age.

Why is the Ohio in my garage
& what man, extinct, tinkered
with its direction?

I will drive the mammoth
out of my garage into a
garden.

I have the courage
to make a point, & if my
point is fluid call me Arrowsmith.

When lost, I invoke on the page
my quarrel with the Beautiful
River.

SEMICONDUCTORS IN THE BREADBASKET

Steamboats in a cornfield.

What they take, took:
bushels of souls.

I see myself as a child. Once a child
always a child,

a towhead among smokestacks.

And there's Lincoln with his stovepipe hat
above the silks

almost coppery in the sunset.

All I survey is corn, the gemstone of the grains.

That is, until Carbon washes over
in shocks.

So curious to find my currency now among stars.

Head in the clouds, the up & up.

A Sudden Unspeakable Indignation

Grasshoppers amass; the fields thick with infantry.

The confederates are expert swordsmen, cutting a swath
of goldenrod with their mandibles.

I, who jaw in the opposite direction, meet them.

My tongue is tungsten.
It obliterates the swarm; it mows down stragglers.

But Manhattan is where steel chokes, tempered.
And thus it blasphemes.

Or so I said to History as she cleaned our terrarium.
But I meant:

Let us say no more of stonewalls, pickets.

THE AMERICANS

Engulfed in dust, the buffalo
overheats, breaks down.
Three red men

tumble out of it & run
in place

hemorrhaging into a roadside. Hand

gestures sign as if on a dotted line,
each A-OK a bullet point
that pings

& trepans among
the deadpan.

Doom remains in their heads
— so much so that one of their hearts

remembers having accelerated.

To think that deserters
mechanical in their movements
are natural enough.

To wander into oasis
& recognize as yet, as good as.

PIONEER

A panhandler holds a cup
designed for hot coffee, &, jostled,
out sloshes a beverage of quarters —
the scissor-tailed flycatcher,
a buffalo on Plains,
& an astronaut who spacewalks —

which means liquidity
for a city of drinkers.

And underneath the downspout
all thirst.

The whale that tipples has always tippled
— this the same leviathan
that swims into the mouth of Seattle,
who was, point of fact,
a teetotaler. Many
the waves

that in their own recklessness
besot those lips.

BROADCASTER

Let's admit that the buzz is sweeter
out of your mouth than mine

& that gold dust is a boon for taste buds

& that when opulence
exits your cave for my hive

it recollects the purple clover
of your palate.

And let's also suppose that your melody is sticky
or stuck

& that honeycombs have collapsed in my rotunda

& you & I have tangled in fluencies
& hum along, hum along.

And let's agree that our drones are killers

& that workers must repose in cells
though hexed

& that we murmur among the mute
& oscillate with the wane.

And let it be said that our Royals were once smeared
with indigo

& that the deft, in response to Depression,

descended into violet,
ascended as ultraviolet.

THE FLUID RIDER

On my nightstand, a seahorse
canters in a glass of water.

It runs in place as if
the beginning is

the end of story.

          . . .

Once upon a time

there was a hippopotamus
in hippocampus...

But I can't
put my finger on it.

          . . .

For whatever Pegasus
that floats

dissolves.

          . . .

But the horse like a hearse
is patient.

Infinitely patient.

The Firmament

Under the stars, a farmer ignites spades
of turf. What is

fire, what is eternal? The
hand of God

immerses the Dipper in trapezoids
of boson, gluon. The farmer feels

a pit in space where flamethrowers confide;
they must be relics. The land,

his near friend, is also his near brother. It asks him
to forget the darkness.

King Salmon

Salmon packed in ice are not swimming, they're saving.
Saving their breath; saving their shekels.

Their gills languish mercurially.
Mouths agape suggest smoking guns.

But eyes look forward — lest cloudy
then fishy.

Sometime in the future the whole mess will transfigure.

They will shimmer in Mercedes.
They will flip-flop at the spa.

Thus, kept on ice as they are, the Kings
save for a rainy day

&, should snow fall, dream of skating
as if to gather up the overcast & sew a silver lining.

In this, they come closest to asking for hands.

The States of the Great Lakes

Here I hibernate in a parking lot,
8° Fahrenheit, my engine resting.
I scan the spaces for another living soul.
Gulls rip the guts out of quietude.

Scavengers that winter in the rustbelt
— what in their hollow bones inspires them?

Such cheats are skilled in the tongue:
like doubletalk, they bullshit & canary.

All fuss. All flak. They beat the air
into puffery. I egg on the clouds
to paint the town; everything is white
& white again.

J. D. SALINGER, RECLUSE, DIES AT 91

The snow is definite & not less definite
for its quickness to melt. Deft as the Snowshoe
the flurry, sleety, runs along the face, the face a fence
&, within, the brain gambols.

Leapers whose nerves were fervent
are not. And yet the light feet were felt. He felt them

in a warren made of weather. There is
blood in the cheek where time has thickened
the mask, & when the saliva has icicled, his pigment
is lost in plaster.

Consider the silence a White Period.

FIGMENT IN PINK & TRANSCENDENTAL

The flamingo
stumbles into a tool shed
next to the weed whacker,
the hoe, the fertilizer, the sack
of concrete
where baby mice nest.

He doesn't see in the dark
but smells the mineral spirits
& the wet ferment
of grass in green clumps
under the carriage of the mower.

And if he lights in the shadows
to get away from the flock
& the Every Good Boy Does Fine
of its treble
then, yes, yes, he'll hide his face.

In the doorframe
his feathers, weird with the perfume
of the estuary, preen;
the wings swing up & down
guarding the way to the garden
like a flamethrower.

May Day

I am adrift in a burned-out canoe
without a helmsman. It was once a birch
straight & narrow made swift. The planets
revolve behind the blue sky, but I don't
witness. The news is good. The willow
has waded into the pond, & the purpose
of the pond is outside of me. The bow
of the boat follows the breezes. Light-
years from Zero.

Nocturnal Movements of the Porcupine

The spiny pigskin flinches.

Winged seeds land on the curvature
that scuttles

like a football

& on these quills they quiesce.

.   .   .   .   .

The porcupine, planted with seedlings,
carries her nursery

out of the dark forest.

The 30,000 or so aspirants clap their hands
because the football moves

in mysterious ways, & under them
an earthquake.

Fish & Wildlife

You catfish at rest on the riverbed are jaguars.

The fawn's ear flicks as she wets her muzzle
but under & deep your whiskers
do not tremble.

Breezes ripple the channel; your gills stock-still.

What will be poached when the upper parts are blues
& swallowtails are forked & the twittering
liquid?

You shadow the mergansers in flotilla
& fanfare.

Thereafter the dunes pummeled with footfall.

The river opens its mouth to hooks.

SHE MAKES ME LIE DOWN

The female Christ swims into lagoon
a stingray, fanning. Gargantuan, she blooms,
skims the sandy bottom, & diamond eyes
cut through the aqua-
naut's valley of coral.

Consider the urchins, how they do not toil.
And the ray, absolving the current, spreads
her rhombic shadow over the contour of the sea.
So feed on frankincense and the diver's sphinx-
like body
laid to rest in a million plankton specks.

The Good Guide, ca. 1310

Spillway of Christ, tempera on wood.
As the pelican tears open its breast

the pear tree yields
12 gold ore miniatures.

Fluent, that's why we admire him —
St. Bonaventure. The fountain

of his blood like a crop sprinkler
erasing gold faces,

fields, & under the fields, taproot.
Apocalypse 22:2.

GEORGE KEATS

How beautiful are the keyholes
in the wrists of brother Keats
who went to America & died
penniless, first arriving in
Cincinnati on a keel-
boat. There is no mention of
the brother in *The Western Spy*
yet we have a letter to John
lamenting a boat that can't be
sold & anticipating a
sawmill to be acquired & boast-
ing of an iron foundry,
the leading one in the West.
Other letters tell of buckeyes
in bloom, bluegrass, bluebirds, swans,
woodpeckers, cranes. He died, but
Isabella, his daughter, was
a girl strikingly free from
morbidity; yet one day she
too lay down to rest on the
sofa in her father's darkened
library, & there set off
the trigger of a rifle,
killing herself unwittingly.
But the story also goes
that she was visited repeat-
edly by a Californian
who took her for walks among
the periwinkles & ivy, walks
that concluded in a visit
to her father's gravesite &
a green cross.

THE LILY ALWAYS HANGS ITS HEAD

The bud of the lily is closed. You

haven't the foggiest idea why. You want it
to soar when deployed.

You want a little zeppelin with propaganda.

To leave behind a paper trail.

The blossom engineered as if with goldbeater's skin
seems close to inflated. Or,

caught up in the atmosphere, fly-by-night.

You look again at the stem. Upon which nods the head
of a Pelican!

And that is how you would leave it if addressed.

But there is always another version. Where the Pelican
sticks out its neck.

LIQUIDAMBAR

This late afternoon among the sweet gum leaves

the nays lag hopelessly behind, mulish,
& no one to feed them.

Go ahead, ask:
where in the leaf pile the negative?

Where in the crown a cavity?

Which of the deadbeats make horse sense?

The sunburned planets, spiky to the lips,
assume a mouth wide open.

Sap in the heartwood whinnies; happiness
exceeds the xylem.

For a moment, only the lacquered time-lapse of the stars
& the wasps

horsewhipped, lamblike.

CRETE

Cast-iron block & tackle;
look for light in an orange boat,
hooks, delphinium,
nets drying in a golden pile.

The marina is open;
it takes Braille to read the cargo.

A supermodel sculls in the harbor,
her high heels dry-docked
as is the schooner.

The fisherman takes apart his propeller in the shade;
both hot & cold the way light treats him.
I said look at the way she treats him.

LINES OF MOTION

Things are said in a great, crow-filled tree,
enough to seed a cloud with black letters.

And the letters are fed to a photocopier
that flashes its curt light upon
the crow-filled tree.

It may be that a painter also eats
of the word, for she stands out
of the picture, painting
the wind.

If so, let the tree accept its position
as vanishing point.

The crown atwitter with the heads
of crows; not crows,
shibboleths.

The cawing creates a causeway
for shibboleths. Who knows
what, what

said who, in a great, crow-filled tree.

CHIAROSCURO

The flea in the unfiltered Chianti
drank & flew out again,
a savvy flea,
a motorized gadfly.

Black on yellow
the silhouettes of children
on a sign that warns traffic to slow
& thus speed up.

And there on the road the shadow
lies in a rhombus;
lies with leaves.

The flea itself a sign,
a flash of sacrosanct. Wherever
it figures, headlights
burn. The flea

slashes at naught with gravity snips.
Giddy. Unhinged.

AUDUBON

You see yourself as you are, & you are
quite surprised at the man with the blowgun
made of river cane. The Beautiful
River is frozen, & you skate across it
chasing after a flock of wild swans. You shoot
a load of thistledown into the birds in question
killing them. On your return, you tie a handkerchief
to a stick, & a band of marauders follows you
like a flock. When, of a sudden, you slip through
the ice & are carried downstream under
the surface, you breathe into your blowgun
a new-fledged man with an aqualung. All
the baleful questions are stuffed in a mouthpiece;
your notes make for a history of overtures.

Heaven

Fieldstone marks the graves
but our names are not engraved. Horses
loosed in the field;

their bliss defends against horseflies
which seem like blackberries
with wings. A tree

grows where there once was
a rudder; the tailpiece
that crash-landed

lost in buttermilk with the Lord
God Birds. With each bird a black box.
And in the box

a transmitter of horseplay. The flight
path was as mazy as
mazy is.

FRONTIERSMAN

In order not to threaten, the naturalist
lies on his back like an astronaut
with legs & arms in the air. An
antelope, cautiously at first,
approaches the spaceman
until it stands over him.
The man makes no
move but imagines
unzipping the underside
of the animal & climbing in.
For he wants to paint the Earth &
what better way to reconnoiter than to
hitch a ride in a rocket. It helps that the ant-
elope is midnight blue; it helps that the flesh
must be gamy. Eventually, he will have to
eat his way out, but by then he will tire
of the atmosphere.

THE REPOSITORY OF SACRED MUSIC

I seek in the electric field
of the cloud a semiquaver
while the weevil
clings to a boll
& hides in it. I listen for
dark matter
— beyond which, space

& the luna
moth that approaches
tentatively an undertone.

A footnote, the weevil
as it fades into tuft
of cotton; catalepsy
approximate to
ellipse of moon.

There is a future. Aircraft
seed the cloud,
&, whatever the motive
of darkness, the light
in the lightning
introverts
as in quietism.

A BETTER MOUSETRAP

Though the mouse opens its mouth
there is no sound. The head
is full of gray space
& the body
careens
as if at the end of momentum.

The mouse is largely apathetic
to greater things, no nose
for news, only a vague
indifference
that tells us it is dead, a dead mouse. For

the alacrity of the feet has ceased, & nothing
suggests that the mouse wishes
to wash the mind
or to wander
its outer banks. The mouse lies

sideways on balsawood like a surfer
& the anticipated waves are
a tongue. We are rightly
afraid of it, though
to insist on
the tongue is to veer lopsidedly.

The Author

A man made of cloud
would have to be unbearable.
His hands & feet likely
devoured by heart,
the most massive star.
He would be very lonely
inside himself. How
sad if he gave up
longhand waiting for the infinite
to be bitten. But we should
not blame History
for a message never
sent. The man is not time-
less; his head perseverates
like a wild pear; his
neck hangs
from a question.
Neither does it seem mealy-
mouthed to ask
for a spear.

FOR LACK OF A BETTER WORD

Afraid in the neighborhood,
afraid in the body,
your tongue pursues the meadowlark,
the hinterlands.

The lark
is not really present there,
not even its tracks, as the artist claims,
but your tongue is as good as a footprint.

Small comfort since the piranha also sleeps
on red velvet, and many terrible winged things
such as seraphim
will follow you to the clearing.

If you could speak plainly
out in the open
you would never paint your tongue.

Notes

Several of the titles in the book are modifications of lines from the journals of Ralph Waldo Emerson, including "Insult Is Necessary for the Perfection of Beauty," "The Calm of a Thoughtful Sentence," and "A Better Mousetrap."

"Aeronautics" borrows a line from a letter of Herman Melville and a description of one of Melville's actual letters, found in *The Writings of Herman Melville*, Vol. 14, *Correspondence*, edited by Harrison Hayford, Hershel Parker, and G. Thomas Tanselle.

"More Splendid" takes its title and first line from a passage in Gertrude Stein's literary portrait of Picasso.

The titles "Andrew Wyeth, Painter, Dies at 91" and "J. D. Salinger, Recluse, Dies at 91" are lifted from the headlines of these men's obituaries in the *New York Times*.

"Darwin's Mouth" refigures a story from Charles Darwin's autobiography, exhibited at the Smithsonian Natural History Museum in Washington, D.C.

"Old World Birds" is adapted from an entry in the 1961 edition of *Birds of the World* by Oliver L. Austin, Jr.

"George Keats" harvests language from a July 30, 1922, *New York Times* article by Felix J. Koch entitled "Tracing the Keats Family in America."

"Lines of Motion" is suggested by Flannery O'Connor's reflections on her own work in *Mystery and Manners*.

"Audubon" stylizes an anecdote from John James Audubon's autobiographical essay "Myself."

"Frontiersman" incorporates a story told by Ben Forkner in his introduction to *John James Audubon. Selected Journals and Other Writings*.

"For Lack of a Better Word" is inspired by the title of a Joan Miró painting, translated as *The Red Disk in Pursuit of the Lark*.

Iowa Poetry Prize and Edwin Ford Piper Poetry Award Winners

1987
Elton Glaser, *Tropical Depressions*
Michael Pettit, *Cardinal Points*

1988
Bill Knott, *Outremer*
Mary Ruefle, *The Adamant*

1989
Conrad Hilberry, *Sorting the Smoke*
Terese Svoboda, *Laughing Africa*

1990
Philip Dacey, *Night Shift at the Crucifix Factory*
Lynda Hull, *Star Ledger*

1991
Greg Pape, *Sunflower Facing the Sun*
Walter Pavlich, *Running near the End of the World*

1992
Lola Haskins, *Hunger*
Katherine Soniat, *A Shared Life*

1993
Tom Andrews, *The Hemophiliac's Motorcycle*
Michael Heffernan, *Love's Answer*
John Wood, *In Primary Light*

1994
James McKean, *Tree of Heaven*
Bin Ramke, *Massacre of the Innocents*
Ed Roberson, *Voices Cast Out to Talk Us In*

1995
Ralph Burns, *Swamp Candles*
Maureen Seaton, *Furious Cooking*

1996
Pamela Alexander, *Inland*
Gary Gildner, *The Bunker in the Parsley Fields*
John Wood, *The Gates of the Elect Kingdom*

1997
Brendan Galvin, *Hotel Malabar*
Leslie Ullman, *Slow Work through Sand*

1998
Kathleen Peirce, *The Oval Hour*
Bin Ramke, *Wake*
Cole Swensen, *Try*

1999
Larissa Szporluk, *Isolato*
Liz Waldner, *A Point Is That Which Has No Part*

2000
Mary Leader, *The Penultimate Suitor*

2001
Joanna Goodman, *Trace of One*
Karen Volkman, *Spar*

2002
Lesle Lewis, *Small Boat*
Peter Jay Shippy, *Thieves' Latin*

2003
Michele Glazer, *Aggregate of Disturbances*
Dainis Hazners, *(some of) The Adventures of Carlyle, My Imaginary Friend*

2004
Megan Johnson, *The Waiting*
Susan Wheeler, *Ledger*

2005
Emily Rosko, *Raw Goods Inventory*
Joshua Marie Wilkinson, *Lug Your Careless Body out of the Careful Dusk*

2006
Elizabeth Hughey, *Sunday Houses the Sunday House*
Sarah Vap, *American Spikenard*

2008
Andrew Michael Roberts, *something has to happen next*
Zach Savich, *Full Catastrophe Living*

2009
Samuel Amadon, *Like a Sea*
Molly Brodak, *A Little Middle of the Night*

2010
Julie Hanson, *Unbeknownst*
L. S. Klatt, *Cloud of Ink*